Overcoming Compassion Fatigue

When Helping Hurts

SHARISE M. NANCE

EXPECTED END

E X

ENTERTAINMENT

Atlanta, GA

DEDICATION

To the caregivers and helping professionals who are in the trenches doing the work you love while building stronger communities-Thank you!!!

To the loved ones of helping professionals and caregivers who remain supportive in this work, this journey-We Thank You!!

To my husband, my rock, William Nance; thank you for your support, patience, understanding, insight and encouragement in my quest to do the work I love and help the helpers.

CONTENTS

INTRODUCTION

Nearly two years ago, I was working full time as a social worker in the community, running a private counseling practice on a part time basis, promoting my first book, exercising 5-6 times per week and newly married! I think it is fair to say my plate was FULL. I had a difficult time removing any of these activities from my schedule as each of them were priorities in my life at the time.

One morning, I had knee pain and could barely walk up and down the stairs. Fortunately, it was a minor knee bruise; nothing 6 weeks of physical therapy and a break from strenuous exercise couldn't fix. A few weeks later, I began to experience pain in my right wrist. Yes, I am right-handed. It hurt to write, it hurt to move or even touch my wrist most days. The surgeon diagnosed my injury as a form of tendonitis, common with women in their 30s. We attempted steroid injections and after two attempts he highly recommended surgery!!!

I remember saying, "I am too busy to get surgery, this could keep me down for nearly 6 weeks!" If I did not get the surgery the injury would not heal on its own. I got the surgery. The toughest part of the process was post-operation, lying in bed with a cast on my arm depending on others and the inability to do what I love-write and help others.

Although I have a strong passion for helping others, I began to question if I still wanted to do this work. A lot of reflection and questioning took place on my part during those 6 weeks. Was I still effective? Did I have the endurance in me to keep pushing? How long could I continue to work full time and run a private practice? Would I maintain my passion for the work I love? I was on Family Medical Leave Act (FMLA) from work and was forced to rest, but that did not stop my mind from working. I remember telling my husband when I recover, I need to write about this experience. My husband's insight into my work-life balance and how I could help others in the helping profession gave me life. I thought about the many social workers, counselors, nurses, teachers, case managers and other direct line workers who struggle with work-life balance, self-care, compassion fatigue and burn out. Initially I wanted to help with work-live balance and self-care. After my personal experiences and witnessing close friends in this profession and colleagues on the brink of burn-out, I began to question "When helping hurts, who helps the helper?"

1
DEFINING COMPASSION FATIGUE

The helping profession can be both rewarding and thankless. The expectations are often high and at times, the compensation is low. I chose this profession 18 years ago, because like many of you I wanted to help. I was (and remain) passionate about assisting those who struggle with advocating for themselves to find and use their voice. We are passionate about taking care of others. We are passionate about alleviating human pain, suffering and trauma. We are passionate about affecting positive changes in families and communities. We get a sense of fulfillment and satisfaction when we help other people.

What happens when this compassion satisfaction turns into compassion fatigue?

Compassion Fatigue is the emotional distress or apathy resulting from the constant demands of caring for others and consistently witnessing pain suffering and trauma. Compassion Fatigue is a serious, yet natural consequence of helping people who are experiencing pain. When we help other people, we have direct contact with their lives. The compassion many of us feel for those we help can affect us in both positive and negative ways.

What about Burnout?

Burnout is reserved for more extreme circumstances. Burnout occurs when one's outlook on life has turned negative because of the impact or overload of their work. The signs and symptoms have become chronic and physical illness has developed. Burnout is frequently experienced in helpers and caregivers. People may end up on extended leave or on long-term disability. It is not uncommon for helpers to experience depression, anxiety or vicarious trauma (when a helper is exposed to the story, emotions and energy a client expresses when speaking of his or her trauma). Remember, we are often in the presence and helping clients in their most vulnerable states. Practicing unconscious empathy while assisting our clients with managing depression, anxiety, trauma and grief is a heavy medicine ball for us to carry on a daily basis.

2
RISK FACTORS FOR
COMPASSION FATIGUE

Mindless (Unconscious) Empathy

Empathy is defined as the ability to understand and share feelings and experiences of another person. The ability to express empathy for someone experiencing pain, suffering and/or trauma is one of the key qualities needed to be effective as a helping professional. There are mindful and mindless ways that we express empathy when helping other. If you do not recognize the dangers of empathy or how to protect yourself from physical and emotional exhaustion, mindlessly expressing empathy can contribute to your levels of compassion fatigue. This can be costly when administering help.

We place ourselves at risk when we engage in unconscious or mindless empathy. Unconscious empathy occurs when we are not present or aware that we are empathizing. The work we do can become harmful when we "catch emotions" as a result of unawareness and the inability to self-regulate. Helping professionals are regularly exposed to a range of various emotions:

- Hope/excitement to hopelessness/anxiety/dread
- Gratitude/thankfulness to anger/range
- Patience to disappointment/frustration
- Joy/triumph to grief/sorrow.

When working with someone in a state of hopelessness, if practicing unconscious empathy, we can absorb their energy and begin to feel sluggish and tired.

The social worker who has been providing services in the community for over 10 years finds herself struggling to survive and thrive in her work. She also struggles to remain present during client meetings. During client sessions she internalizes the client's depression, anxiety and is unaware when or how this process takes place. She continues to go through the day on auto pilot barely managing her caseload.

The caregiver who is responsible for attending to the needs of an elderly parent, family member and/or children finds herself or himself consumed with both fear and guilt about circumstances beyond their control. She assumes 100% responsibility for the success, failure and ultimate well-being of her loved ones. Boundaries and limitations often become blurred with most caregivers when the person on the receiving end of the help is a loved one. Some of the most popular statements caregivers have shared that express their fears and guilt include: "I feel guilty if I am not always available and accessible to my loved one." "What happens if I am not there to help when they needed me most?" My biggest fear is my father falling down the stairs and not being there to help him." "No one can care for my parents, children the way I can." "I owe it to my parents to be their primary caregiver." These statements are filled with emotions, thoughts and beliefs that come from a powerful place. As helping professionals and caregivers, we must get clear about our role in our client, patient and/or loved one's life.

What am I responsible for?

_____

What are my clients and loved ones responsible for?

_____

What is in my control?

_____

What is outside of my control?

_____

Oftentimes, our stress levels increase allowing compassion fatigue to settle in when we over-identify with our clients and/or oved one's. Over-identifying with our clients can place us into a rescuer role, believing we are 100% responsible for other people.

Nature of the Workload

The greater number of people on your caseload who have experienced pain, suffering and trauma combined with your beliefs of your role and the expectations from the organization can have an impact on the development of compassion fatigue.

Imagine the case manager who has a caseload of 50 clients, who have combined diagnoses of chronic illness, PTSD, complex trauma, grief and anxiety; with an agency expectation of meeting with each client weekly and meeting the daily documentation requirement. This case manager is also the sole provider of his elderly parents and has little to no support from other family members. Many of us find ourselves in the role of helper in both our personal and professional lives. It is imperative that we understand our role in each situation. Helping your clients and loved ones identify additional supports outside of just you can prevent compassion fatigue, burnout and allow you to enjoy the work you love.

Number on Caseload _____

Identify additional supports available to client/loved ones

_____

_____

_____

_____

Supports available to you

_____

_____

_____

_____

Clinician/Helper/Caregiver vulnerability

You are human, so it is likely that past learning experiences can positively and negatively impact your work with clients and loved ones. Further, if you have a personal trauma history, you are more vulnerable to vicarious trauma. "Research shows that mental health professionals have a higher rate of ACEs than non-clinical professionals (Elliott & Guty, 1993)." The fewer supports and positive coping skills you have available to you, the more susceptible you are to vicarious trauma, compassion fatigue and burn out. It is imperative to develop a healthy self-care regimen to remain present while doing this work.

Self-Care: Self-care is not a selfish act, but a necessity and priority, especially when you are in the business of helping others manage their emotions. Many of us become overconsumed with helping others and self-care is often neglected. You cannot pour from an empty vessel. If you cannot take care of yourself by properly nourishing, resetting, re-centering and rejuvenating you become more susceptible to compassion fatigue.

3
PROTECTIVE FACTORS FOR COMPASSION FATIGUE

Conscious (Mindful) empathy

Conscious empathy is fully feeling and experiencing another person's emotions while being fully grounded in your own being. You are self-regulating while empathizing. You can observe their feelings with no attachment and allow space between their pain and your well-being. "I feel your pain, but this pain does not belong to me." "I will treat this pain as a visitor by observing, accepting and letting it go". When we are intentional about practicing conscious empathy, we are more equipped to help heal others.

How do I practice conscious empathy?

Being comfortable with emotional pain. "Get comfortable with being uncomfortable" is a quote that resonates with me when thinking of the work we do. Sitting with someone else's emotional pain is uncomfortable. To ease this discomfort, many helpers either overcompensate by taking 100% ownership for managing their client's emotional pain or perpetuate the problem by helping clients avoid or escape their emotional pain. An example of a helper escaping a client's emotional pain includes celebrating more than anyone when a client appears to be free of the emotional pain. On the surface, it appears the helper truly cares but underneath this care lies joy from being released of the anguish of their client's emotional pain. This can be saddening and invalidating to clients as it sends the message that as the helper "You cannot handle when I am sad." "You don't like it when I am sad because it makes you sad." We must get comfortable with our own pain before we can accept other's pain. Until we can accept our clients' and loved ones' pain, we cannot help them heal. When we overcompensate or join clients in escaping their emotional pain, we place ourselves in the role of rescuer; doing more harm than help. "The better we take care of ourselves and maintain a professional separation from our clients the more we will be in a position to be truly empathetic, compassionate and useful to them." (Rothschild, 2006). We can reap the rewards of compassion satisfaction when we practice conscious empathy.

Awareness (of Negative Thoughts):

When we are experiencing distress, our minds may look for potential threats or danger to keep us safe. When your thoughts lead to frustration, anger and blaming, negative thinking patterns can begin to settle in. The following strategy can help you interrupt the cycle of negative thought patterns and reduce stress.

Questions to assess your current thoughts?

- Am I expecting perfection from myself and others?

- Am I overestimating setbacks, obstacles or tragedy?

- Am I blaming or criticizing myself or someone else for something that isn't entirely my fault or his or her fault?

- Am I concentrating on my shortcomings and neglecting to celebrate all of my strengths and accomplishments?

- Am I setting unrealistically high standards for myself and others?

- Am I jumping to conclusions and assuming I know how something is going to turn out?

- Am I getting stuck in black and white "all good or all bad" thinking without checking for other possibilities?

Which thought patterns do you use most?

_____

_____

_____

_____

_____

_____

Identifying these negative thinking processes gives us insight into our cognitive distortions and beliefs and is the first step to preserving compassion satisfaction.

The Power of No

N-o is arguably the most powerful two letter statement. Many helpers struggle with using this statement as it can feel like we are not helping or allowing someone in distress to experience more stress. When we say no, we are setting boundaries for ourselves, clients and loved ones. We are teaching them how to respect us, themselves and others. We are also teaching our clients and loved ones the meaning of staying true to their values and principles. By no means am I minimizing the challenge of saying no to your loved ones and clients. Getting more comfortable with saying no is a process. We must have patience with ourselves during this process as we are not going to undo years of rarely saying no to others to being comfortable saying no to a parent, boss or client overnight. We entered the helping profession because we care. You are committed to this profession because you care. You commit extra time tending to your parent, child with disability or other family member out of love and care. Love and care are tremendous strengths and only become weaknesses when this love and care comes at the expense of your own health and wellness. You deserve to "put your own oxygen mask on first." Taking care of you is the best gift you can give to yourself and your loved ones. Let's explore what happens to your body when you say no.

Take a moment and practice saying say "No" "No thank you" "No I cannot" "I cannot make a visit to you today as your appointment was scheduled for Tuesday." "I cannot drive you to your doctor's appointment. Let's take the time to explore the other supports and resources available to you. I have full confidence that we can get creative in finding other long term solutions." "If you are experiencing a crisis, let's revisit your crisis plan and follow up during your appointment." "My caseload is full and taking on another case will take away from my effectiveness with clients." "I need to take care of myself for now, so I will have to decline your offer, thank you for thinking of me."

Take a moment to reflect and then write down what happens to your body when you say no.

_____

_____

_____

_____

_____

_____

The Overcoming Compassion Fatigue workshop will provide you with the motivation as well as useful strategies to say no to people in a respectful manner and the next steps when saying no doesn't work.

Values

Core values are the fundamental belief of a person (or organization). These guiding principles dictate behavior and help us distinguish between right and wrong. Core values also help us determine if we are on the right path and fulfilling our goals by an unwavering guide. Some examples of core values include:

Accountability	Being liked	Community
Creativity	Achievements	Caring
Competition	Discipline	Ambition
Collaboration	Control	Education
Empathy	Equality	Excellence
Faith	Family	Friendship
Honesty	Integrity	Independence
Individuality	Innovation	Interdependence
Intimacy	Justice	Knowledge
Leisure	Loyalty	Money
Patience	Prestige	Success

Take a moment to write down 3-5 most important values to you:

_____

_____

_____

_____

_____

These values will guide you in challenging situations. When faced with difficult decision, ask yourself, "does this align with my values?" Being unclear, fuzzy and or compromising your values leads to stress and dissatisfaction. We are happiest when our lives are consistent with highest values and innermost convictions. We enjoy working for companies that uphold our values. Get clear about what you believe in and what you stand for and do not deviate from these values.

"It's not hard to make decisions when you know what your core values are." Roy Disney

Self-Worth

Self-worth is defined as the sense of one's own value or worth as a person. We tend to feel good about ourselves when we do good work and when we help our clients make positive changes. How is your self-worth directly linked to compassion fatigue and burn out? Sitting with people in their most vulnerable moments and assisting them in managing their emotions is challenging. It is imperative that we have a strong grasp on who we are, our role in our client's life and awareness of our thoughts, emotions and physical sensations in reaction to those challenging moments.

How do you feel in those moments when you are helping people?

_____

_____

_____

What kind of thoughts are you having when you are helping people?

_____

_____

_____

What physiological responses do you experience when helping people?

_____

_____

_____

These questions will guide you through those difficult sessions where you may have missed something, client regresses or does not get better. Taking the time to reflect on your self-esteem throughout the day is imperative, especially in those moments when you think you are doing more harm than good to clients. Self-esteem is fluid, it is not a fixed state and some days will be better than others. A helping professional in the first year of their career will probably not have the level of self-esteem in their skills and clinical judgment as a more seasoned professional. The situations you encounter daily have an impact on how you view yourself. Each day and each client are unique and having the experience can bolster our self-esteem. To maintain healthy self-esteem, remember to take frequent breaks to assess how you are feeling about yourself, how you are being influenced by your client's situations and redirect negative thoughts.

4
COMPASSION AND SELF-COMPASSION

Compassion is defined as the emotional response to someone who is experiencing pain accompanied by a strong desire to alleviate their suffering. Compassion is one of the main qualities helping professionals share. It requires unique skills, abilities and qualities. Attributes of compassion include sensitivity, distress tolerance, non-judgement and empathy. Studies have revealed when we express compassion oxytocin and opiates are released which lead to trust, soothing and calmness. Other benefits include stronger immune system, lower blood pressure and cortisol levels, improved mental health and decreased risk of anxiety and depression. Most, if not all helping professionals begin their career in the Zealot phase, full of excitement (this concept discussed further in the Compassion Fatigue workshop). Helping professionals can quickly find themselves in a place of withdrawal or irritability when encountering the barriers to compassion. The barriers to compassion include heavy caseloads, documentation, lack of resources, as well as the strong feelings that may be triggered when working with clients. These feelings can include hopelessness, inadequacy, self-doubt and fear that may cause you to question your competence in your area of expertise. Although many of us may experience barriers to compassion when working with our clients; showing compassion is typically as automatic as breathing for many helping professionals, while practicing self-compassion on a regular basis is an area in which many of us struggle.

Self-compassion is awareness of our pain, suffering and shortcomings without judgment and follow through with action. Benefits of self-compassion includes, but not limited to perspective taking, forgiveness and altruism, improved relationship functioning, reduced emotional reactivity, reduction in perfectionism and rumination, less negative affect and more acceptance. Barriers to self-compassion can include feeling selfish, negative thinking patterns, non-supportive work environments, non-supportive relationships, low self-worth, criticism instead of compassion curiosity (a perspective that draws us from our involvement in repeating habitual patterns of misperception to a place where we can understand our lives with the compassion to explore with an open heart to a place of inner peace and expansion).

Self-compassion includes the recognition of what is happening to us and giving it a name. Instead of "shoulding" all over ourselves by saying "I should have done more," "I should have caught that;" we reframe our thinking (in the same way we do with our clients to help them view their situation through a broader lens) name the behavior and show kindness to ourselves. Shifting our self-talk to "I felt overwhelmed today and had a challenging day." "Today may have been a challenging day and challenging days happen, tomorrow will be better." When we practice self-compassion by reframing our thinking and normalizing our mistakes; we are relating to ourselves with a greater awareness of our own suffering. We must remember to treat and speak to ourselves in the same manner we would treat our clients and loved ones. Most importantly, we must have patience with ourselves when practicing self-compassion; remembering this too is a process which requires daily intentions and non-judgment during our struggles.

5
STRESS-MANAGEMENT=SELF-MANAGEMENT

Stress is a response that the brain activates to meet a demand or threat; often referred to as the fight, flight or freeze response. The stress response is a process the body enters by signaling hormones and systems to react to a crisis or challenge. Stress is caused by stressors. For example, taking an exam or fear of failing an exam causes a lot of anxiety for many. The test is the stressor as it is the event that is casing the stress. The body's reaction to this stressor is the stress response; this response includes physiological responses such as a change in heart rate, blood pressure muscle tension and a release of stress hormones. Most of us are fully aware of what happens to the body under stress. I know this because I have witnessed many colleagues provide education to clients on this topic. However, as helping professionals, we often struggle to recognize when our bodies are under stress. We also face ongoing stressors in our lives such as high demands at work, financial concerns, family and intimate relationship conflicts. When we can recognize our stressors and the stress response that follows, we can learn how to better manage stress and anticipate situations that are likely to trigger stress; thus, decreasing our likelihood of experiencing compassion fatigue.

Take a moment to reflect on your stress response and warning signs. Awareness is the first step to long-term success with stress and self-management.

Some signs of the Human Stress Response include but are not limited to:

Fight, flight or freeze response, muscle tension, gastrointestinal symptoms (nausea, slow digestions, irritable bowel symptoms) hyperarousal (sharpened senses, increased blood pressure, rapid heart rate.

What are the first three things you notice when you are stressed?

_____

_____

_____

Self-management is a key component to managing stress levels and will also guide you throughout your day when helping clients manage themselves. It involves setting goals as well as managing time and energy. Many of us invest time developing treatment plans with our clients to focus on goal setting and timetables for achieving those goals. This written plan is a working contract between the clinician and the client that clearly states specific, measurable, attainable, realistic and timely (S.M.A.R.T) goals. How many of us have invested the time to develop and commit to a personal self-care/self-management plan? I have also neglected the importance of my self-care needs. Let's break that trend today by developing a written self-management plan and sticking to it. It is imperative that we also utilize the S.M.A.R.T criteria while creating our plan.

My Self-Management Plan:

Physical:

Exercise: How many days per week can I commit to 30 minutes of aerobic exercise (walking, jogging, cross training, etc)?

_____

_____

_____

Sleep: How many hours of sleep do I need per night to function at a high level each day? What time will I go to bed? What time will I wake up in the morning?

_____

_____

_____

_____

Nutrition: What do I need to do to eat more balanced meals throughout the day? When will I go grocery shopping? How often do I need to meal plan throughout the week? Do I need a budget for dining out?

_____

_____

_____

_____

Professional:

What are my professional boundaries with clients, co-workers and management? What are my negotiables, non-negotiables and "no-big deals" as it pertains to my professional boundaries?

_____

_____

_____

_____

How much time and resources will I commit to investing in my professional development each quarter (i.e books, conferences, seminars, supervisions, coaching)?

_____

_____

_____

_____

Personal:

What are my personal boundaries with friends and family? What are my negotiables, non-negotiables and "no-big deals" as it pertains to my personal boundaries?

_____

_____

_____

_____

How much time and resources will I commit to investing in my professional development each month or quarter (i.e self-help, journaling, retreats, creating vision-board/vision board parties, vacations, exercising)?

_____

_____

_____

_____

Spiritual:

What can I do to address my spiritual needs (Prayer, meditation, organized religion, yoga, self-reflection, volunteering, finding a spiritual mentor, etc)? How much time per week can I commit to these activities?

_____

_____

_____

_____

Psychological/Emotional:

What can I do to address my psychological and emotional needs (Daily positive affirmations, journaling, joining a support group, self-reflection, practice asking for help, identifying positive support system, seeking counseling, etc)? How much time per week can I commit to these activities?

_____

_____

_____

_____

Remember, this is your working self-management plan meaning there is flexibility to make changes as needed. In the manner that we do monthly treatment plan reviews with our clients, I encourage weekly check-ins to hold yourself accountable to attending to your self-care needs.

6
SIGNS AND SYMPTOMS OF COMPASSION FATIGUE

Signs and symptoms of compassion fatigue can affect the whole person. In Charlene Richardson's Caring Safely program; she discusses how the symptoms of compassion fatigue manifest themselves physically, emotionally, spiritually and behaviorally.

Physical:
- Rapid Heartbeat
- Difficulty breathing
- Pain
- Headaches, dizziness, stomach aches
- Dread of working with certain clients
- Decreased sense of purpose/enjoyment in career
- Diminished feelings of work competence

Emotional:

- Anxiety
- Depression
- Hopelessness
- Helplessness
- Anger/Rage
- Shutdown
- Numbness
- Hypersensitivity
- Emotional rollercoaster
- Overwhelmed
- Depleted

Spiritual:

- Loss of purpose
- Anger at GOD
- Questioning spirituality or religion
- Lack of self-satisfaction
- Questioning the meaning of life
- Cognitive:
- Confusion
- Distracted
- Diminished self-esteem
- Intrusive thoughts of clients or personal situations
- Apathy
- Disorientation
- Rigidity
- Self-doubt
- Perfectionism
- Thoughts of self-harm or harming others

Behavioral:

- Sleep disturbances
- Moodiness
- Impatient
- Withdrawn
- Appetite changes
- Irritability

Interpersonal:

- Decreased sex drive
- Mistrust
- Social isolation
- Difficulty separating work from personal life
- Projection of anger, fear or blame

Source: 20 Quick Strategies to Help patients and Clients Manage Stress (2015) Charlene Richardson

7
PREVENTION

Workshops:

This book defined Compassion Fatigue. Workshops will offer tips and strategies for managing and preventing Compassion Fatigue in a supportive setting with other caregivers and helping professionals

Workshops range from 1.5-5 hours depending on needs.

The workshops will help the helpers/caregivers:

- Identify and implement the parallel process of healthy boundary setting and self-advocacy from practitioner to client.

- Identify where they are in the compassion fatigue trajectory and how to remain consciously empathetic when helping clients and loved ones.

- Identify and manage client related stressors.

- Manage distress and negative thoughts.

- Practice self-compassion to increase compassion satisfaction.

- Implement Acceptance and mindfulness strategies.

- Implement Grounding techniques.

- Identify and implement nourishing and non-negotiable self-care activities.

*For more information on workshops, contact us at vitaminchealing@gmail.com

Needs Assessment:

After facilitating various workshops for social service and non-profit organizations in 2017, I recently conducted an anonymous survey via social media with the purpose of bridging the gap of communication between management and direct line staff to aid in the prevention of compassion fatigue. The survey targeted 61 helping professionals who were asked some of the ways middle and upper management can support direct line workers.

The results revealed:

- 19.67%: Including mental health days in PTO (Paid Time Off) Packages

- 29.51%: Ensuring decision makers and those promoted to management positions have relevant experience as direct line workers

- 26.23%: Investing in regular self-care activities for staff

- 8.2%: Create and maintain dialogue to track compassion fatigue

- 16.39%: Other (Monitor staff caseloads, regular and

reflective supervision that does not turn administrative, authenticity/transparency by upper management, increased pay, all of the above)

Counseling:

Helping can hurt when we neglect our own self-care needs, fail to work through our personal traumas and/or transference and countertransference issues. You do not have to suffer alone or in silence. Helpers need help too as we are not exempt. If you are in the Pittsburgh or surrounding areas, contact HandinHand Counseling Services, LLC, outpatient mental health counseling for assistance in addressing these areas.

10 Duff Road Suite 201
Pgh, PA 15235
412-871-5391
www.hihcounseling.com
info@hihcounseling.com

Other Mental Health Resources:

• National Alliance on Mental Illness (NAMI):
1-800-950-NAMI info@nami.org
M-F, 10 AM - 6 PM EST

• National Hopeline Network:
1-800-SUICIDE (784-2433)

If your depression is leading to suicidal thoughts, call the National Hopeline to connect with a depression treatment center in your area. The Hopeline also offers a live chat feature for those who don't want to (or are unable to) call and can dispatch emergency crews to your location if necessary.

National Suicide Prevention Lifeline:
1-800-273-8255

Trained crisis workers are available to talk 24 hours a day, 7 days a week.

Re:Solve Crisis Network (Allegheny County residents)
1-888-796-8226

Trained crisis workers are available to talk 24 hours a day, 7 days a week. Mobile crisis team is also available.

8
CONCLUSION

In conclusion, the purpose of this book was to serve as a resource and shed light on the much-neglected topic of Compassion Fatigue. The combination of information provided in this book followed by the workshops; can assist you in the unique experience within the journey of surviving and thriving in the work we love to do as helping professionals and caregivers.

Remember, you are not alone when experiencing the range of emotions that come along with this work. Again, the work we do is both rewarding and challenging. Achieving, regaining and maintaining compassion satisfaction is an ongoing process which requires patience with yourself as well as being intentional about working toward healthy self-care practices.

It takes the combined efforts of a supportive management team along with a competent, inspired and motivated direct line staff equipped with the knowledge and tools to prevent compassion fatigue.

I wish you success in your selfless mission to uphold the integrity of the helping profession. To quote author and teacher

Jack Kornfield, "If your compassion does not include yourself it is incomplete."

9
TESTIMONIALS

"Sharise is by far one of the most humble, welcoming, and clinically-grounded mental health professionals that I've ever worked with before. Her ability to take therapeutic information and share it with audiences in an informal and down-to-earth way are second to none.

Our organization called upon Sharise to deliver a workshop on self-care for our participants and she was nothing short of phenomenal. After the engagement, attendees shared how warm and soothing the environment was for them. We understand that the spaces we serve in are only as safe as our facilitators allow them to be; and Sharise ensured that everyone was comfortable that evening.

With that being said, I give Sharise the highest recommendation for her expertise, services, and commitment to helping others through therapy."

Julius A. Boatwright, MSW, LSW
Founder + CEO | Steel Smiling
www.SteelSmilingPGH.org
"Our Stories Matter"

"Sharise Nance was a powerful asset to the 1st Annual Love Wisdom & Empowerment Women's Conference! Her presentation was captivating as she delivered practical tools and tips that ladies could implement immediately, to assist them in embracing their purpose!

Sharise is a skilled communicator, her authenticity captured the hearts of the audience, they walked away with plenty of gems! I greatly appreciate the value that she brought to my women's conference and look forward to working with her in the near future!"

Founder & Ceo Serene Motivations, LLC
Johnnette Young-Lewis

"Family Resources would like to thank Sharise Nance of Handinhand Counseling Services, LLC for her awesome workshop on Self-Care in the Workplace. Her book Walking the Tightrope of Life gave staff great resources and real-life insight on how to practice self-care."

ABOUT THE AUTHOR

Sharise Nance is a Licensed Clinical Social Worker, Speaker, Award-Winning and Best Selling Author. She is the co-owner and founder of HandinHand Counseling Services, LLC and has 18 years of experience working with a diverse population of children, families, adults and couples. She is also the founder of Vitamin-C-healing, an organization that provides services to non-profit organizations, social service organizations, helping professionals and caregivers struggling with self-care, compassion fatigue, burn-out and work-life balance. Sharise presents national keynotes, workshops and seminars for young professionals, helping professionals, entrepreneurs, parents and adolescents. She has facilitated workshops on Compassion Fatigue for Healthy Start, Inc, Family Resources of PA, Westmoreland County Area Agency on Aging, University of Pittsburgh, and Auberle. She has been featured on local TV shows, national podcasts, local radio shows and local newspapers. Sharise was also honored locally in 2015 for an Entrepreneur of the Year Award in the Social Service profession and won a second place award for Vitamin C Healing for the Mind, Body and Soul in the self-care/medicine category from the Author's Zone 2014 Pittsburgh Author Awards. The Vitamin C Healing for the Mind Body and Soul Healing Workbook recently won author of the year in the health and wellness category of the 2017 Indie Author Legacy Awards in Baltimore, Maryland. Walking the Tight Rope of Life: Refuel Renew Re-Center Your Work Life Demands also won a second place award for the self/care category for the 2017 Pittsburgh Author Zone Awards. Sharise resides in Pittsburgh, Pennsylvania, with her husband.

Printed in Great Britain
by Amazon

21370597R00031